RITES AND MEDITATIONS

PAUL MURRAY

Rites and meditations

THE DOLMEN PRESS

RITES AND MEDITATIONS is designed by Liam Miller, typeset in IBM Journal Roman and printed in the Republic of Ireland by Patternprint Limited for the publishers, The Dolmen Press, Mountrath, Portlaoise, Ireland.

First Published 1982

British Library Cataloguing in Publication Data

Murray, Paul
      Rites and Meditations
      I. Title

      ISBN 0 85105 393 9 *Pbk*
      ISBN 0 85105 402 1 *Spl. edn.*

© 1982: Paul Murray

CONTENTS

1

2

Office of the Dead

3

Meditations

ACKNOWLEDGEMENTS

Some of the poems in the first part of the collection
were originally published in *Hibernia, New Irish Writing
(The Irish Press)* and *The Lace Curtain.* The first twelve
poems are from *Ritual Poems* (New Writers' Press:1971).

Office of the Dead: The poem "Tenebrae" from this
sequence was first published in *The Lace Curtain* No. 5,
Spring 1974; "Vigil" in *Younger Irish Poets* (Blackstaff
Press); "Lauds" in *Playing with Fire: A Natural
Anthology of Religious Poetry* (Villa Books); "Prime"
in *Choice: An Anthology of Irish Poetry* (The
Goldsmith Press); and "Compline" in *Era* No. 5, 1980.
Acknowledgement is made to the editors of these
publications.

To
Henrique Rios

1

INTROIT

This morning,
on entering the cold chapel,

       I looked first
to the sun, as the pagan does,
not by strict custom
nor by constraint, but because

       I too, as creature,
sense man's primitive emotion:
his need to praise.
And so, like priest or pagan,

       according
as the sun moves, I perform
this ancient ritual.
And though not always able

       to approach,
often, effaced in light, I stand
before this
chalice of the morning,

       I break this
ordinary bread as something holy.

THE RITUAL

Imagine now the dead, and how
Beside her coffin priest and lover stood.

Imagine how, crossed over wooden beads,
Her fingers, drained of life, achieved
Within his eyes (the man she loved)
The shape of perfect prayer; within
The other's heart, despair.

Imagine now the dead, and how
Beside her coffin priest and lover stood.

Imagine how she held the jewelled
Symmetry of pain; and how, throughout
The ritual, within his heart, he
Saw the golden crucifix become
Bright jewels glittering.

POSSESSED

Whose name is Legion speak.

Was it a shadow merely sang
Under him the stroke
Of burning seed;

Who fathered him his sight: was
It the phoenix bird winged
Giddy over flame ?

Who have possessed him, answer:

How in the empty socket of his eyes
Appeared the brilliant sun,
Twice over.

FEAR

this is my fear,
that I who have observed
the beauty of an insane woman
time after time, appear
to imitate her ritual; the water
she has carried within
cupped hands
I cannot hold. Into the thin
and delicate vessel of poetry
live water spills.

THE VISIT

I

The glass door opens
into the dream,
the threshold .
I have come face to face with her
again - High Priestess -
Her tall, almost motionless
emaciated figure . . .
She, into whose quiet radius
and orb, each day
I bring small tokens of my charity:
fresh fruit and flowers.

II

Tonight, transfigured in her room's
cracked mirror,
- cobwebs in her eyes - trailing
her ceremonial robes of purple eiderdown,
she moves blind fingers
to the glass -
like some huge moth
her body trembling violently.

Darkness covers her face.

She is beginning to scream
softly. Door opens.
The night-nurse enters quietly.
It is past the hour
for visitors.

I say nothing. Silence.
(My eyes are full of pity)
I am beginning to feel
awkward, charitable.
As visitor, it is permitted only
that I smile and appear normal.

III

At a distance,
passing along the empty
corridor, I may be permitted
to observe the final Ritual:
night-duty, the Public Ward;
beside each bed
fresh fruit and flowers.
Most likely I will say prayers
as for the dead. I will pass
by the vault
where each asylum creature shrills
to his cracked star.

Is it impossible, I wonder: is it
impossible to know
how far
beyond the reach of human mind,
through which unknown, luminary sphere
her mind is spinning?
                    I reach out . . .
her hands are thin grey clouds shivering.

DEATH OF A PRIEST

Only afterwards, when flesh succumbed
And he could feel his last
Breath freeze against her cheek,
And somewhere, in the distance, chorus
Contra chorum, could hear
The De Profundis plead for him,
Was he afraid.

A black breviary propped between his
Chest and chin, a cold
Hand closing his eyes, touching
Without chrism his wrinkled forehead;
Only then could he believe
She was neither fantasy of daydream
Nor temptation: Death.

WIDOW

Certainly as children we never thought
of them as lovers.
She moved within the compass

of his needs and turned to him
so naturally.
There was always time

to make his quiet unobstrusive
fate her own,
gradually to be woven

into the pattern of his changing moods
and even to accommodate unchanging
fears like waking up

alone in hospital, - she'd stay there
half the night just watching him.
Without direction now,

awkward among her married
sons and daughters, she comes and goes
like Santa Claus.

OLD PHOTOGRAPH

Incredible that I should
find your photograph so unfamiliar,
Father. I do not mean the loss
of memory, but that, however gentle,
you were always firmly
in command -
         never this old,
half-smiling, vulnerable gentleman.

DEPARTURE

From the platform, all I could see clearly
Was a dark profile of her face,
Awkwardly framed within the carriage window.

She was wearing a small mantilla of white lace;
Dark hair fell to her shoulders.
At first, what drew my attention was something

Quiet, like sadness, although I noticed how she
Smiled vaguely when a group
Of late-comers entered the same compartment.

Seconds later, they too became aware, when
Suddenly, face pressed against
The window, she stared, as if trying

To focus her eyes on some tiny familiar
Figure - momentarily visible -
But then lost among the crowd, shrinking

Like those around him on the platform, unable
To stand still, finding
Himself forced back into the empty station.

A KIND OF PALMISTRY

We were not superstitious; this medium
was simply our first way through
to each other:

You, telling my fortune, and I, feeling
your small hot palm
make love to my fingers.

It was little more than friendship.
Though once, appearing
to take my adolescent life-line

Seriously, you spelt out unmistakable
meaning, auspiciously
suggestive at the time; and yet,

By virtue of my conscience intervening
never so favourable an omen
less prophetic!

AUNT JANE

And to think we had expected
A great lady; suddenly, there
She was, peering incredulously over the hedge,
Wiping her spectacles, wondering if we were
Really her nephews and nieces.
Her arrival made nonsense of our
Childhood mythologies:
Aunt Jane carried within her brown
Plastic suitcase a handkerchief
Containing real tears.

Later we discovered also: one glass
Bottle, stuffed with cotton
Wool and pink sedatives; one small
Bottle of cough mixture (half empty);
Several faded copies
Of the Reader's Digest; and from
Her youngest son, who lived
Somewhere in the Far East, "with much love"
From his wife and three children,
A giant Christmas Card.

RAIN

At the third hour always
the same dream - suddenly
I am a child again. My eyes are opening
slowly . . .
        At the entrance leading
to the cemetry of the dead
I am carrying a golden crucifix.
Above my head, invisible
among the trees, rain whispers endlessly.

At the fourth hour always
the same three Sisters
praying:
each with the same voice
saying the same prayers.
        Always
the same girl (golden-haired)
dead in her coffin.

At the fifth hour I am beside the grave.
Altar-boy.
I am made of stone (pink marble)
My thurible is black.
        If I close
my eyes, only two facts remain
unanswerable: why incense, sprinkled
over charcoal, smells so sweet;
and why, above my head, invisible
among the trees, rain whispers endlessly?

2

OFFICE OF THE DEAD

Grant us extraordinary grace,
O Spirit hidden in the dark in us
And deep;
And bring to light the dream out of
Our sleep.

David Gascoyne: *Kyrie*

Dedicated to the Memory
of Peter Duignan O.P.
Conleth Cronin O.P.
and
Austin Clarke

VIGIL

Out here all day by myself,
the sky, dull since late morning,
sunless . . .
the first drops of rain on my forehead;
in my eyes for the first time,
for an instant,
the slow-moving and grey canopy
of cloud, blanched by sheet-lightning . . .
If now, at this moment,
high above me around the tower
and walls, against the roof,
I hear what shakes the sudden-trembling
earth, and feel across my brain
sky's thunder break . . .
Or if, in the silence after darkfall,
I am slowly nearing the gate
where the path stops -
later, at a time I do not expect,
in a dream, or standing in Choir, head
bowed, lips christening the air
with canticles, I fear inside my brain
the memory of thunder, dream's gate
half-opening into nightmare . . .

TENEBRAE

I

eve of the year's turning,
the winter solstice.
to be awakened by voices crying
in our sleep.
           in obeisance, shadows
at the gothic window.
their arms, spread close to the earth.
their voices
           slow chiming of bells
becoming louder.

out of the darkness, god
has hurled fire. live
smoke in our nostrils. ashes
upon our faces
           and on our hands
(the damp earth floor is shaken)

inside the chapel tower
infinitesimal echoes. choir stalls
are empty. shadows
and no candles. dry rot.

these walls are alive with rumours . . .

as if finally to open
our eyes might not illumine more than our fears,
 (clouds laden with stars, night's passage
into a dream of silent rooks,
the weariness of nightfall)
                              this dream,
unless we waken earlier than usual,
the ancient dead shall hail as their sole
heritage:
            primeval dark wherein no candles burn,
            unhallowed shrine,
            familiar paradise to which
they shall return, bearing on thin shoulders
dead wood;
            familiar orchard
            threshold of limbo
            unreal magnificent asylum.
as it was in the beginning,
ourselves also
                  as witnesses,
standing amazed before the silent threshold.

to speak therefore of the shades' elysium, let us say
we are asleep or at prayer,
that we do not remember.

III

asleep or at prayer.
                        eyes glazed
with staring at saint maelruain's tree
(the spine's collapse)
                        we who have thrown
far out of mind the golden disc . . .

these images
before they are shadowed over
before we are shadowed over:

aureole of lightning. thunder
in the veins of maelruain.
                        black rain.
(whether asleep or at prayer
we do not remember)

                     for such dead
as these, god's tongue speaks blasphemy.
nor shall his thunder cease,
nor we explain limbs splayed
                     like an octopus.
saint maelruain's tree has fallen.

LAUDS

All things the Lord has made, O bless the Lord,
Give glory and eternal praise to Him . . .

Together with our morning papers' dead:
unsmiling heroes, war-jaded, no longer game, the old,
the maimed, you also, your stoic gaiety
now needed more than ritual,

O bless the Lord.

And you, and you also,
crazed victims of unnatural love, chained to
the masks of vampire or sacrificial dove,
the tortured and the torturer,

O bless the Lord.

And you, who have no fear
of those who crush the bone, your innocence inviolable;
stone angel, prostrate in your mother's womb,
unwanted three-months' miracle,

O bless the Lord.

And buried behind charitable walls,
the unseen, unmourned for, you, your voices ever singing
in the darkness, cherubim of dwarf and mongol, bright
galaxy of souls of Limbo,

O bless the Lord.

And you, the hideously mourned, lips
parted, rouged, smiling under expensive oils, O Dives,
when through the painted mask
your lips are burned,

O bless the Lord.

30

And you, when on your brow there glows
the desolate mark of Cain, when in your eyes, in the temple
of your heart, only the towering and dead
effigies of God remain,

                      O bless the Lord.

And you, whose memory revives
after the serpent sting: eyes closed, imagining your soul
redeemed, re-entering the lost kingdom. Exile,
when Death shall prove your dream,

                      O bless the Lord.

And you, those dying under ritual of torture
or no ritual : the suicides, the uncremated spirits in the fires
of Purgatory and Buchenwald - O quiet, innumerable
souls facing unquiet doom,

now, out of the burning fiery furnace,
out of the heart of the flame,

        give glory and eternal praise to Him.

PRETIOSA

Small lights and candles
burning in the dark,
O teach us not to be
so much absorbed by grief,
but soon to laud and praise
the ordinary burning light
which fills
      and flames
the chalice of the morning.

PRIME

What requiem shall the Choir sing?
Other than the need to overcome despair,
Somehow to give order to this thing,
What use our ritual? What prayer
Can breathe back breath, restore those lying
In the conscience of our city? At night, gunpowder
Flames above the asphalt. Only the sirens sing.

TERCE

O God come to our aid.
Each day, at each hour,
the dust of your living Word
is on our lips.
We are neither living nor dead.
O Lord make haste to help us.

We are neither living nor dead.
Each day, at the same hour
of Terce, or at the fixed hour,
under the same frail cover
of ritual,
we shoulder our fears and our dead.
Each day, minute to minute,
hour to hour,
we pray and do not pray,
We face and cannot face
without aid,
without grace,
the spaces above and between us.

Each day, minute to minute,
hour to hour,
the clay is under our feet.
Minute to minute, hour to hour,
the wings beat
over our head: the echoes,
the small fears picking to thread
our souls' embroidery . . .

And nor is the heart,
And nor are the loins invulnerable.

O God come to our aid.
Each day, at each hour,
the dust of your living Word
is on our lips.
We are neither living nor dead.
O Lord make haste to help us.

SEXT

Whether in my place now
minutes before the hour of Sext,
or still out here in the open, walking
back and forward under the trees,
I have again become absorbed,
it seems, by tracing, re-tracing
an almost pilgrim journey
back into my mind - somewhere,
between fiction and memory,
turning, returning again to find
the mud paths of the Culdee.

NONE

Soon we must weave and weave
a new pattern . . .
                    Each day, the door
into the same chapel closes behind us:
we are neither living nor dead.
Each day, at each hour,
the same small fears are picking to thread
our souls' embroidery -

Weave, we must weave and weave
a new pattern.

Soon, on the dark
pillows of the air, we who are
neither sleeping nor awake,
neither living nor dead,
shall we not feel the silent pressure
of the Dead,
hear their impenetrable whisper?

Silence and be silent . . .

From the earth and from the air,
before they are shadowed over,
before we are shadowed over,
we who are neither living nor dead
must weave and interweave the Dead
into our lives, and the Living,
the new and the live thread -
weave and weave a new pattern.

VESPERS

Late again for Vespers! The last hour
So much absorbed, abstracted, that now as if helpless alone
To shield my eyes and lips from images and the power
In tongues, I wait to hear the ritual monotone
Of Vespers; my brothers' choral psalmody echoing
From the Church, re-echoing along this passageway
To draw my footsteps forward. Listening,
I thumb the pages of my breviary yet do not pray.

Inside, aloof above our sanctuary and Choir,
Stained glass remains contemplative, disdains my brother clerics'
Loud vernacular. Unmoved by centuries of change, there
Blessed Catherine reaches out her arms, eyes open, fixed
Upon her Saviour crucified. There too, arbiter
Of reason's doubt, soul's certainty, before his crucifix
And medieval God, St. Thomas, though he gazes where
All contraries unite, foresees men damned beyond the Styx.

The Choir singing, "But with you is found forgiveness . . .", I pass
Back into the Cloister of the Dead. Here,
Silence needs no rule; stained glass,
Heavy with light, sensual, flames quietly. Here,
To do penance, win plenary indulgence
For those in torment, Dominicans of former years
Took off their shoes, walked barefoot round the Stations,
Fasted, prayed, until by custody of eyes, lips, ears,

Desiring only to drink the bitter cup, those able
Would experience Christ's blood flowing
Through their veins. And now, whereas we do not have such ritual
Or faith, each day we know Christ makes the hour of dying
Ceremonious, we taste His cup. And though time spent at prayer

Seems vain, each day we pray and hope, our own breath
Failing, this smallest grain of incense, these threads of smoke,
Though faint like spilled perfume, may sweeten our bitter death.

COMPLINE

Peace after ritual . . .

After our last slow procession
back into cloister,
leave no-one to mourn the Dead.
Close and bar the doors,
extinguish the votive candles.

Later, when only the tall white
tapers of memory burn into the dark,
silently gladly
O may the Dead take back
into their arms our requiem.

3

MEDITATIONS

Death: What are you waiting for?
Knight: I want knowledge.
Death: You want guarantees?
Knight: Call it whatever you like. Is it so cruelly
              inconceivable to grasp God with the senses?
                      Ingmar Bergman: The Seventh Seal

My heart has five other senses of its own. These senses of
my heart view the two worlds.
                      Jalàlu'l - Dìn Rùmi: The Teachings

I

Not the slow drum beating
in the heart, the music
in the blood. Not step by step
led forward through the dark
palpable medium of the senses.
And yet, at the beginning notes
of truth, when at last the tired
dislocated strings of the spirit
have been wound back into place,
a new stroke of rhythm, a new music
begins to quicken in my pulse,
begins to waken out of sloth
to a lover's discipline
both my disjointed sense and thought,
until with no other guide,
no other plan except that inner throb
and cadence in my blood, I am drawn
out into the darkness towards you.

II

In the body God is present, the body
in His temple. In the body the appearance
of His light is like a cave illumined,
or like a lamp when it is lifted upward
into a dark niche, and the lamp
is encased in a glass, and in the lamp
the oil, which rises to a flame
and burns, is neither from the East
nor from the West; and, in the trembling
interspace between one jet of flame
and the surrounding void, the plain
crucible of glass is radiant with fire
and is the sole mediatrix of light.

III

With those friends who disclaim all knowledge
of God, I boast and I say,
                        "I know Him",
and I say I am speaking from my own experience.
But my friends say: "Be reasonable, how
can you know Him, how can you be so sure
that you are not self-deceived?" This question,
I know, is honest; and I know it demands
for an answer not these obscure words
about experience, but the clear evidence
of a man's life. However, I will say it
here again, and even to my own doubting heart,
and to my five agnostic senses: "I know Him".

IV

Every instant, with every tongue, God
whispers His own secret
into the ear. Every moment, to every
eye, He reveals His own beauty.

From the beginning until the ending,
He, the Lord, is silent. He is the one
Lord of silence. And yet, every instant,
is it not by His Word the living stream
rises under the earth? At every instant,
in every place, does the same Word
not speak to all the senses of the mind?

From the beginning until the ending,
He, the Lord, is hidden. He is enclosed
in darkness upon darkness. And yet, even
now as the snow is falling, in the calm
and slow transfiguration of the pathway
and of the mountain, does His own Angel
of Radiance not shine and tremble?

Every moment, in every aspect, but
darkly, God whispers into the ear
His own secret. He reveals each being
to itself as His own witness.

V

Lord, you are
        to me
a sword of division, at once
full of wisdom and full of wilfulness.
Nonchalant in your manhood,
but in your Godhead, jealous
as a lover -

O loss of myself.
O whirlwind in my heart.

VI

At first, only the feeling, the awareness
of a vast distance between myself, my own
life, and His life. But then,
gradually also, the interior conviction
of His memory: the make-belief
and the belief of being myself a witness
to the ordinary and extraordinary events
of His life.

   The knowledge that His history means
more to me now than my own memory
of the past, and the pressure of that memory.
The fact that His presence being recalled
is even more true, more real
than the unconscious memory - in my bones
and in my blood - of my own mother's womb's
shape and pressure.

   The knowledge that at the last when I
open my eyes, He will be there, that I
will see Him through my eyes and hear Him
in my ears, and touch - even with my own
hand - the Word who is life.

VII

Sometimes when I speak to you,
                              Lord,
my friends tell me I am foolish, or that
I am dreaming. And maybe
they are not completely mistaken. For it is
true that you have given me a life
which is a kind of sleep,
and that everything I now perceive
appears for the most part
                              like a dream.
And so, "Yes", I will say to my friends, "He
is, of course, part of my dream, but then
I am part of his dream, too".

VIII

"Listen, O listen", He said, "Even the sharp
wounds you have known - and the bitterness -
the tears you have wept out of shame
and disillusion, each one I have counted; and
trembling, but not with anger, not with hate,
I have placed them on your life's thread."
   "O dark Lord", I answered, "if thus according
to Your will the knotted shapeless thread
of time can be unwound, and thus the myriad
worlds of men are told like beads in Your hand,
now, though You have called me, and will
call me again into the hearts' cell of solitude,
Your name, O dark Lord, and all the praises
of Your name, I will repeat, over and over.

IX

Not the naked sudden thought
of this or that lovely girl,
the sudden impulse, the desire to take
into my arms for a brief moment
the sensual, midnight spouse.
Not that which in the mind is natural
to imagine, natural to affirm: the most
ordinary, most obvious answer
to a grown man's fullest need.
Not that calmness therefore, not even
with the trembling of desire appeased,
that dark spontaneous joining together
in one flesh, of man and woman,
that brief perfect equilibrium.
And yet, at times, I know that in my
being you have touched me, Lord:
the stark passion of desire
is calmed, and calm is passionate.

X

To raise up from the ground my whole being
and my life; each day, with my hands empty,
and my heart empty, to stand, and to look
towards the one source of all.

   To be able to accept the hour of knowing
and of unknowing, to be able to be passive.
And though not yet by this or by that vow
made naked in my intent, to be, through time,
by one desire, one gift, made careless
of every covering and of every cloth. Not by
atonement of will, but by His power, to be able
to lie down passive like Michelangelo's Adam.

   O to feel, at the tip of my finger, God's
suddenly live pressure, that same merciless,
merciful lightning of God's hand.

Notes on *Office of the Dead*

When this small sequence of poems was begun
(c. 1970), it was still common practice to refer to the
hours of the Divine Office by their original latin titles.
Since that time, the form of Choral Office and even the
individual names of the hours have been slightly revised.
For my own convenience, however, and also I suppose
as a kind of "memory" I have chosen to name each poem
and hour by what would have been its original latin title.
Exception has been made only for *Vigil*, the title of the
first poem in the sequence.
The epigraph, "Grant us extraordinary grace . .", is taken
from *Poems 1937-42* by David Gascoyne. I am grateful to
Poetry London for permission to quote.

Note on *Tenebrae*
The poem, a dreamprayer of the Dead, is enacted
around St. Maelruain's Tree close to the Dominican
Priory in Tallaght. This tree, which in popular legend is
said to have been planted by Maelruain an austere Celtic
monk of the ninth century, has once or twice been
struck to the ground by lightning.

Note on *Lauds*
In form, the poem corresponds to a canticle sung
usually at Lauds. This canticle was taken originally
from the Book of Daniel and was first heard on the lips
of three young Israelites cast into a burning *fiery
furnace* by King Nebuchadnezzer. (Dan 3:51-90).

Note on *Terce*
*O God come to our aid, O Lord make haste to help
us* - the short versicle and short response with which
almost every hour of the Divine Office begins.

Note on *Sext*

    Culdee - a reference to the ninth century Celtic monks who lived in Tallaght on the site of our present Dominican Priory.

Note on *Vespers*

    Blessed Catherine - the Dominican mystic and saint, Catherine of Siena.

    St. Thomas - Thomas Aquinas, the medieval Dominican theologian.

    But with you is found forgiveness . . . - a line from the *De Profundis* psalm sung at Vespers in the Office of the Dead.

Note on *Compline*

    Our last slow procession . . . - the Salve Procession which leads from the central aisle of the Church back into cloister. In the Dominican tradition, it concludes Night Prayer or Compline and marks the end of the day's Office.

*

Note on *Meditations*

    A small number of phrases and images have been freely adapted from certain eastern and western poets and religious authors. At first, my plan had been to make a list of these sources. But I have now decided to print the poems by themselves without "scholarly" appendix. It would, in any case, I am afraid, embarrass and put to shame these ten short meditations to place *underneath* them, as it were, in footnotes, the names of poets whose lives and whose works "one cannot hope to emulate".